GLORIA STEINEM

By Jacqueline Laks Gorman

WORLD ALMANAC® LIBRARY

Please visit our web site at: www.worldalmanaclibrary.com
For a free color catalog describing World Almanac® Library's list
of high-quality books and multimedia programs, call 1-800-848-2928 (USA)
or 1-800-387-3178 (Canada). World Almanac® Library's fax: (414) 332-3567.

Library of Congress Cataloging-in-Publication Data

Gorman, Jacqueline Laks, 1955-
    Gloria Steinem / by Jacqueline Laks Gorman.
      p. cm. — (Trailblazers of the modern world)
    Includes bibliographical references and index.
    Summary: A biography of the feminist writer and activist, founder of Ms. magazine and the Ms. Foundation,
and her impact on the women's movement.
    ISBN 0-8368-5093-9 (lib. bdg.)
    ISBN 0-8368-5253-2 (softcover)
    1. Steinem, Gloria—Juvenile literature. 2. Feminists—United States—Biography—Juvenile literature.
3. Women—Biography. [1. Steinem, Gloria. 2. Feminists.] I. Title. II. Series.
HQ1413.S675G67   2003
305.42'092—dc21
[B]   2003042285

First published in 2004 by
World Almanac® Library
330 West Olive Street, Suite 100
Milwaukee, WI 53212 USA

Copyright © 2004 by World Almanac® Library.

Project manager: Jonny Brown
Editor: Jim Mezzanotte
Design and page production: Scott M. Krall
Photo research: Diane Laska-Swanke
Indexer: Walter Kronenberg

Photo credits: © AP/Wide World Photos: cover, 25 top, 26, 27, 39 top, 43 bottom; © Bettmann/CORBIS: 6, 13, 16, 17
top, 19, 25 bottom, 29, 34; © Lisa Blumenfeld/Getty Images: 42 right; Copyright Bettina Cirone; Sophia Smith
Collection, Smith College; 36; © CORBIS: 43 top; © George De Sota/Getty Images: 37; © Owen Franken/CORBIS: 24;
Copyright Gisele Freund, Sophia Smith Collection, Smith College: 28; © Hulton Archive/Getty Images: 4, 14, 15, 17
bottom, 18, 20, 22 both; Copyright Liberty Media for Women; Sophia Smith Collection, Smith College: 39 bottom;
Copyright Ms. Magazine; Sophia Smith Collection, Smith College: 31; Copyright 1972 Ms. Magazine; Sophia Smith
Collection, Smith College: 41; NASA: 42 left; Copyright People Weekly; Sophia Smith Collection, Smith College: 5;
© Robin Platzer/Getty Images: 40; Smith College Archives, Smith College: 11, 12; Sophia Smith Collection, Smith
College: 10, 33; Toledo-Lucas County Public Library: 8; University of Toledo Archives: 7 both

Printed in the United States of America

1 2 3 4 5 6 7 8 9 07 06 05 04 03

TABLE of CONTENTS

Words that appear in the glossary are printed in **boldface** type the first time they occur in the text.

CHAPTER 1

CHANGING THE WORLD FOR WOMEN

As recently as the late 1960s, women in the United States were expected to be happy homemakers, content with marriage, child care, and housework.

In the late 1960s—not so long ago—the life of the average American woman was quite different from what it is today. Women were expected to leave their jobs (if they had jobs) at a young age to marry and have children. At home, they were responsible for taking care of the children and performing all the housework. Women were not supposed to be doctors, lawyers, police officers, firefighters, engineers, or business executives. If women did have jobs, they were paid much less than men, and newspaper want ads were divided into "male" and "female" categories. A woman could not apply for a credit card or car insurance unless her husband signed the application.

Women's lives were different in many other ways, too. The terms "**sexual harassment**," "date **rape**," and "battered women" did not exist, even though the problems themselves certainly did. If a woman wanted to end a pregnancy, probably her only option was an illegal and potentially dangerous **abortion**. There were no women astronauts, no women justices on the Supreme Court, and only a handful of women in the U.S. Congress.

Gloria Steinem played a huge role in changing the lives of women. Modern **feminism** has had many important pioneers, but Steinem has been one of feminism's most outstanding organizers, leaders, and spokespeople. As the force behind Ms. magazine and as a speaker and writer, she has helped make the world a better place for women, one step at a time.

The modern feminist movement began in the late 1960s, and Ms.—the world's first mass-market feminist magazine, created and run by women—played a crucial role in its development and impact. Before Ms. first appeared as a special insert to New York magazine in December 1971, Steinem had already been lecturing about feminism around the United States. After her lectures, women would ask her questions about issues such as affordable child care, education for older women, improving working conditions in factories and offices, and organizing local women's groups.

Steinem and other feminist activists realized that women needed a national **forum** to receive and exchange practical information, air their views, and learn what other women were experiencing during a time of drastic social change. Ms. magazine became that forum. The magazine supported and helped shape the feminist movement.

As the inspiration for Ms., as well as one of the

Gloria Steinem's work as a writer, speaker, and force behind *Ms.* magazine did much to change the lives of women.

Ms., Not Miss or Mrs.

The feminist magazine *Ms.* appeared at a time when most women were referred to as "Miss" or "Mrs."—titles that clearly indicated marital status. The preview issue of the magazine explained:

"*Ms.* is being adopted as a standard form of address by women who want to be recognized as individuals, rather than being identified by their relationship with a man. After all, if *Mr.* is enough to indicate "male," then *Ms.* should be enough to indicate 'female.' . . . The use of *Ms.* isn't meant to protect either the married or the unmarried woman from social pressure—only to signify a female human being. It's symbolic and important. There's a lot in a name."

magazine's founding editors, Steinem became for many the voice and symbol of the feminist movement. She helped bring feminism into the mainstream of American life—no easy task, given the intense opposition feminists often faced, from men and women alike. Today, Steinem continues to be a fierce defender of the causes and concerns of women.

Steinem (center, holding sign) and other feminists lead thousands of women in a 1979 march against *pornography* in New York City. Feminists said pornography exploited women and encouraged violence against them.

Traditional Women's Magazines

When *Ms.* was first published, mainstream women's magazines, such as *McCall's* and *Ladies' Home Journal*, printed articles on food, fashion, and beauty. These magazines followed a formula first established by *Godey's Lady's Book*, the most popular women's magazine of the nineteenth century. The magazine mostly featured articles on fashion and homemaking. It avoided controversial topics of the time, such as slavery and women's *suffrage*.

Gloria Steinem believed *Ms.* would be different from traditional women's publications because it would be about "not how to make jelly, but how to seize control of your life." It featured articles on subjects such as reproductive rights, sexual harassment, violence against women, and the politics of housework. With the success of the feminist movement, many of these subjects have become common in mainstream magazines, but they were once highly controversial.

A CHALLENGING CHILDHOOD

Gloria Marie Steinem was born in Toledo, Ohio, on March 25, 1934. Her childhood was far from traditional, and it was often difficult. Her father, a resort owner and traveling salesman, was an undependable parent, given to wild schemes and frequently in debt. Her mother was emotionally disturbed and suffered from severe depression and anxiety. The hardships Gloria faced as a child, however, ultimately contributed to her becoming a caring, passionate adult.

FAMILY BACKGROUND

Gloria's parents, Leo and Ruth Nuneviller Steinem, met while working on the college newspaper at the University of Toledo. They married in 1921 to the dismay of their relatives, since their backgrounds were so different: Leo was from a wealthy Jewish family, while Ruth was from a working-class Christian family. Ruth briefly taught school, then worked as a reporter, editor, and columnist for a Toledo newspaper. She continued this job after the birth of her first child, Susanne, in 1925. Five years later, however, Ruth suffered her first mental breakdown, which involved a stay in an institution. She never practiced journalism again.

Leo, meanwhile, tried his hand at the entertainment business. In 1925, he had

Gloria's parents, Ruth (above) and Leo (below), met as students at the University of Toledo.

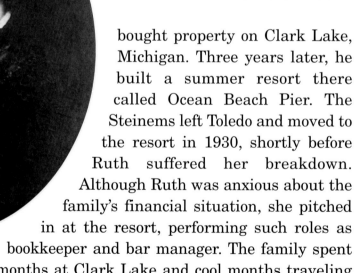

Gloria's grandmother, Pauline Perlmutter Steinem, was active in feminist causes. Gloria did not learn about her history until many years after the woman's death.

bought property on Clark Lake, Michigan. Three years later, he built a summer resort there called Ocean Beach Pier. The Steinems left Toledo and moved to the resort in 1930, shortly before Ruth suffered her breakdown. Although Ruth was anxious about the family's financial situation, she pitched in at the resort, performing such roles as bookkeeper and bar manager. The family spent warm months at Clark Lake and cool months traveling in a house trailer to places such as Florida and California, where Leo bought and sold antiques. This pattern continued after Gloria was born in 1934.

Gloria and Susanne rarely attended school. Instead, Ruth taught them. The girls enjoyed their unusual life. Gloria later remembered their times at Clark Lake as "a great time of running wild, catching turtles and minnows and setting them free again, looking for coins that customers at my parents' dance hall dropped in the lake, wearing a bathing suit all day long." She even learned how to tap dance from one of the resort's cigarette girls.

CARING FOR HER MOTHER

The Steinems' unsettled life, however, was too difficult for Ruth. She and Leo separated in 1944 and divorced a year later. Leo took off for California, while Susanne began attending Smith College in Northampton, Massachusetts. At first, Gloria and her mother lived near the college campus. Then they moved back to Toledo, where Gloria entered the sixth grade.

For the next six years, Gloria cared for her mother, first in the basement of a rooming house, then on the upper floor of the house Ruth had inherited from her parents. The physical conditions were awful, and the house was in such poor shape that it was difficult to rent out the first floor. The furnace often didn't work, and sometimes there were rats. But the emotional conditions were worse. "I knew my mother loved me, but that she couldn't take care of me," Gloria later said. Indeed, Ruth could not take care of herself. She frequently took medication for her illness and lay in bed hallucinating, listening to inner voices. As Gloria wrote years later, "She was a loving, intelligent, terrorized woman. . . . In many ways, our roles were reversed. I was the mother and she was the child." Gloria shopped, prepared meals, and cleaned the house, as well as a child could.

She escaped the harshness of her life by reading, going to the movies, and listening to the radio. She also danced in community clubs and performed in shows. A tall, striking girl, she even entered a local beauty pageant and a talent contest. Gloria liked to pretend that she had been adopted and that her real family would one day come to find her.

As a teenager in Toledo, Gloria danced in community clubs and performed in local shows.

"Ruth's Song"

Shortly after Ruth Steinem died in 1981, Gloria wrote an essay entitled "Ruth's Song (Because She Could Not Sing It)." In this essay, Gloria looks back at her mother's troubled life. At one point, she describes the moment when she realized as a child just how ill her mother was:

I made a last stab at being a child. By pretending to be much sicker with a cold than I really was, I hoped my mother would suddenly turn into a sane and cheerful woman bringing me chicken soup. . . . Of course, she could not. It only made her feel worse that she could not. I stopped pretending.

CHAPTER 3

BEGINNING A NEW LIFE

In 1951, the church next door to Ruth and Gloria offered to buy their ramshackle house, so the house could be torn down and an addition to the church built. Leo and Susanne came to Toledo to discuss Ruth and Gloria's future. Susanne had graduated college and was living and working in Washington, D.C. She asked Leo to care for Ruth for a year, so that Gloria could finish high school in Washington. Leo was reluctant but finally agreed, and the house in Toledo was sold.

A new life began for Gloria. Leaving Toledo—and her mother—meant that Gloria could socialize more, get involved in extracurricular activities, and work harder in school. She graduated high school in June 1952 and in the fall entered Smith College, the same school her sister Susanne had attended.

Gloria (second row, sixth from left) and some of her Smith classmates outside their dormitory

The Seven Sisters

In the 1950s, Smith College was one of seven prestigious, all-female colleges considered to be the equals of all-male Ivy League schools such as Harvard, Princeton, and Yale. Known as the "Seven Sisters," the schools—Smith, Barnard, Bryn Mawr, Mount Holyoke, Radcliffe, Vassar, and Wellesley—were all founded in the nineteenth century, when providing high-quality educations to women was considered revolutionary. The Seven Sisters set high standards for their students and expected they would use their educations for further achievement in the world. Only five of the schools are still all-female; Vassar now admits men as well as women, while Radcliffe merged with Harvard in 1999.

Gloria loved Smith College. She was away from her family for the first time and was in the company of smart, interesting young women. She also knew that a good college education meant she would escape the fate of her less fortunate Toledo friends, who were destined to become the wives of factory workers in their working-class neighborhood. College was "a path first to an interesting job and ultimately to a better class of husband," Gloria later wrote. (Like most young women at the time, she assumed she eventually would get married.) Marriage, however, was in the future. For now, college for Gloria was a safe shelter, a wonderful place "which served three meals a day and gave me as many books as I wanted to read."

Her classmates regarded Gloria as somewhat exotic. Tall, witty, and beautiful, she could help them with practical skills, such as ironing their clothes and applying makeup. She also told wonderful stories and gave thoughtful advice. In return, they helped her with subjects such as fine arts and French. "This cheerful bargain was the beginning of an important lesson," she wrote in Glamour magazine in 1964. "Don't worry about your background; whether it's odd or ordinary, use it, build on it."

Gloria's 1956 graduation photo from Smith College

Gloria had an active social life, and during her senior year she became engaged to Blair Chotzinoff, a wealthy and handsome Air National Guard pilot. She worked hard at her studies, and in June 1956, she graduated magna cum laude with a degree in government, having been elected to the honor society Phi Beta Kappa. She was also awarded a fellowship to travel and study in India. This opportunity allowed Gloria to break her engagement. Getting married after graduation was the expected step for Smith students, but Gloria was not the average "Smithie." She loved Blair but believed marriage was the wrong path for her at that time.

AN UNWANTED PREGNANCY

Gloria first traveled to London, England, where she worked while waiting for the visa she needed to enter India. To her horror, she discovered she was pregnant. She knew that Blair would marry her if she told him, but she also knew that she could not face the prospect of marriage and motherhood. In England, a woman could get a legal abortion if two doctors agreed that the pregnancy would endanger the woman's health. Gloria managed to find two doctors to sign the necessary papers,

Anti-abortion protesters demonstrate outside the U.S. Supreme Court in Washington, D.C. Today, abortion remains a highly controversial issue.

The Abortion Issue

Until the 1970s, abortion was illegal in most of the United States. A few states did allow abortions, but only if the pregnancy endangered the woman's life. Abortions were not permitted for victims of rape or *incest*. If a woman wished to end a pregnancy, she could travel to a country where abortion was legal, but this option was costly and time-consuming. The only other alternative was an illegal abortion. Many women died or suffered permanent injury from illegal abortions, which were performed in secrecy and usually under unsanitary, dangerous conditions. Abortion did not become legal in the United States until an important U.S. Supreme Court ruling in 1973. The procedure remains a highly controversial issue. Some people support a woman's right to an abortion, while others oppose it for moral or religious reasons. Today, access to abortion has become more restricted, and abortion opponents continue to seek new rulings by the Supreme Court against the procedure.

and one of them performed the abortion. "I never forgot the weeks of panic before I found a doctor, or how it changed my life to be able to continue the trip to India that was about to begin," she remembered years later. At the time, however, she told no one, and she did not speak of the abortion until some fifteen years later.

EXPERIENCING INDIA

Gloria finally received her visa and arrived in India in early 1957. She immediately became enchanted with the country, which she thought was exotic and mysterious. Gloria attended classes at the University of Delhi, filed the reports required for her fellowship, and wrote a guidebook called The Thousand Indias for the government tourist bureau. She also darkened her hair and began wearing a sari (a traditional Indian dress) so she would fit in better with the local people. Setting out alone to explore India, she traveled by bus and third-class railroad car. She came face-to-face with the reality of India's poverty and hardship.

Gloria visited a retreat run by followers of the late Indian leader Mahatma Gandhi. At the time, members of India's different **castes** were clashing in violent riots. In an attempt to stop the riots, teams of Gandhi's followers walked from village to village, talking to people and urging landowners to give some of their property to the poor. Gloria joined one of these teams. She was especially useful, because village women would not attend meetings unless another woman was present. The teams walked miles each day, eating and sleeping with the villagers they met. "I found there was a freedom in having no possessions but a sari, a cup, and a comb, and, even in the

Women collect water from a village well in India in the 1950s. Gloria's visits to Indian villages helped make her more aware of poverty and social injustice in the world.

Mahatma Gandhi and His Beliefs

Mahatma Gandhi (1869–1948) fought against injustices in Indian society and helped lead India to independence from Britain in 1947. As a proponent of nonviolent protest, he tried to achieve political and social reforms peacefully, without fighting. After Gandhi was assassinated, in 1948, his followers continued to spread his words and live by his teachings. One such follower was the leader of the team Gloria joined when she walked from village to village in an effort to end the caste riots of the late 1950s. Gloria learned several lessons from the leader, just as he had learned them from Gandhi:

If you want people to listen to you, you have to listen to them.

If you hope people will change how they live, you have to know how they live.

If you want people to see you, you have to sit down with them eye-to-eye.

Indian leader Mahatma Gandhi (center) inspired many followers with his belief in change through nonviolent protest.

midst of turmoil, a peacefulness in focusing only on the moment at hand," Gloria recalled years later. "I remember this as the first time in my life when I was living completely in the present." Gloria stayed with her team until blisters on her feet became infected, and a doctor ordered her to stop.

In 1958, Gloria returned to the United States determined to write about politics and social issues, such as poverty. She settled in Cambridge, Massachusetts, where she worked for the Independent Research Service, a nonprofit group that encouraged American students to attend world youth festivals. Gloria would not learn until years later that the group was funded by the Central Intelligence Agency (CIA), a federal agency that uses secret operations to collect information on other countries. At the time, the CIA was interested in the youth festivals because they were largely dominated by **communists**.

CHAPTER 4

MAKING A NAME IN NEW YORK

Steinem moved to New York City in 1960 to become a writer. Her first job, with a humor magazine, led to her meeting many influential people in the journalism world. One such person was Robert Benton. Now an Academy Award–winning screenwriter and director, Benton was then an art director for Esquire magazine.

He encouraged her to write articles for a variety of magazines. Steinem did so, and her first major article appeared in Esquire in September 1962. Called "The Moral Disarmament of Betty Coed," it examined the effect of the new birth control pill on college women. Soon, she was writing regularly for magazines such as Glamour, Vogue, and Ladies' Home Journal, mostly interviews with celebrities and features on fashions. She also socialized with many New Yorkers who were, or would soon be, famous in the theater and music worlds.

Steinem with one of her boyfriends, Herb Sargent, at a 1966 New York benefit. Her active social life was often chronicled in the gossip columns.

TRYING TO BE TAKEN SERIOUSLY

Much as she enjoyed her life, Steinem wanted to write about more important issues. Her editors suggested she go undercover as a Playboy Bunny at New York's new Playboy Club, so that she could investigate the discrimination and sexual harassment the women faced. Steinem's report was published in two parts in the May and June 1963 issues of Show magazine. Although she wrote sensitively about the Bunnies' awful working conditions, the article made her famous for a different reason—she had dressed up as a Playboy Bunny. Despite its strengths, the article did not lead to her finding other important assignments.

Steinem wanted desperately to be regarded as a serious journalist, and she wanted to write about the social causes with which she had become increasingly involved—**civil rights**, the efforts of the United Farm Workers union to gain rights for **migrant** grape pickers, the war in Vietnam, and the presidential campaigns of antiwar candidates. (In the mid-1960s, she had little interest in the new and growing women's movement.) But the causes she believed in and the subjects she wrote about were vastly different. In 1963, for example, she participated in the civil rights March on Washington, but she also wrote The Beach Book, a lighthearted resource guide for sunbathing.

Dressed as a Playboy Bunny, Steinem does undercover research for a magazine article.

Steinem helped bring public attention to the plight of migrant farm workers. Here, labor leader Cesar Chavez (second from right) leads a march urging people to boycott lettuce.

A CELEBRITY IN HER OWN RIGHT

The public knew very little about Steinem's intelligence and commitment to social causes. Yet by the mid-1960s, she had become well-known in the gossip columns as a

glamorous, beautiful young woman with an active social life. In May 1965, she was even profiled in Newsweek in an article called "News Girl," which stated: "Usually

The Turbulent Sixties

The 1960s were a stormy period in U.S. history, as social tensions that had been growing for years finally exploded. One controversy was the civil rights movement. African Americans had long been denied equal rights, especially in the South, where they were often not allowed to vote and were forced to use separate public facilities, such as restaurants and swimming pools, and attend separate schools. Civil rights leaders such as Dr. Martin Luther King, Jr., led protest marches demanding equal rights and encouraged boycotts of businesses that discriminated. King called for nonviolent protest, but a militant "Black Power" movement also arose, sparking riots in many cities. Many college students, meanwhile, protested against U.S. involvement in the Vietnam War. A feminist movement also emerged, as more women realized they were being treated unfairly— even within the civil rights and student antiwar movements.

Protesters demand equal rights for African Americans during the March on Washington in August 1963. The civil rights movement was one of the most important developments of the 1960s.

the journalist remembers his place—on the edge of the action recording the news made by others. But Gloria Steinem, a striking brunette of thirty, is as much a celebrity as a reporter and generates news in her own right."

In 1968, Clay Felker—whom Steinem knew from their work together at Esquire—founded New York magazine. Becoming the magazine's contributing editor and political columnist, Steinem was able to write about meaningful issues. Finally, she wrote, "my work as a writer and my own interests began to combine." That year, she covered the U.S. presidential campaign and interviewed African-Americans in the Harlem neighborhood of New York City after the assassination of Martin Luther King, Jr.

Betty Friedan

Betty Friedan was born in Peoria, Illinois, in 1921. In 1963, she wrote *The Feminine Mystique*, a book that transformed many women's lives and may well have launched the modern women's movement of the 1960s. In the book, Friedan noted that many middle-class women were bored and frustrated with their lives as homemakers, even though society insisted they should be content and fulfilled. She wrote, "We can no longer ignore that voice within women that says: 'I want something more than my husband and my children and my home.'" Friedan told women they should take control of their lives and demand full, rewarding roles in society as the equals of men. In 1966, she helped found the National Organization for Women (NOW), which sought to bring women equal opportunities. Friedan was also the first president of NOW.

Betty Friedan, whose book *The Feminine Mystique* helped launch the modern women's movement in the United States

CHAPTER 5

FEMINIST AWAKENING

By 1969, Steinem was a well-known journalist committed to a variety of social causes. Yet thus far, she had not been involved with the new women's liberation movement. Then, an incident occurred that made her a feminist at last.

A SPEAKOUT ON ABORTION

In early 1969, the state of New York was considering changes to its abortion law. Hearings were held, but few women were called as witnesses. To protest the way the hearings were conducted, a group of feminists known as

Women in the late 1960s demonstrate for safe, legal abortions.

the Redstockings held a "speakout" in a New York City church, where women stood and spoke about their personal experiences with abortion. Steinem was in the audience covering the speakout for New York magazine. She did not talk about her own abortion but was deeply affected by what she heard. "I had had an abortion when I was newly out of college, and had told no one," she later wrote. "If one in three or four adult women shares this experience, why should each of us be made to feel criminal and alone? How much power would we ever have if we had no power over the fate of our own bodies?"

Listening to Other Women

In her book, *Outrageous Acts and Everyday Rebellions* (1983), Steinem looked back at the 1969 speakout on abortion, which caused her to become a feminist:

*I sat in a church basement listening to women stand before an audience and talk about desperately trying to find someone who would help them . . . being asked to accept **sterilization** as the price of an abortion, and endangering their lives in an illegal, unsafe medical underground. It was like the "testifying" I had heard in Southern churches and civil rights meetings of the earlier sixties: emotional, rock-bottom, personal truths. Suddenly, I was no longer learning intellectually what was wrong. I knew.*

After the speakout, Steinem wrote her first article about feminism, "After Black Power, Women's Liberation." In it, she predicted that "a long-lasting and important mass movement would result" if the middle-class reformers from the National Organization for Women (NOW) joined with younger, more radical women who were concerned with issues such as rape, child care, and welfare reform. She wanted to write more about feminism, but her male editors urged her to focus on "real" issues, such as politics, instead.

"THAT WAS THE BEGINNING"

For Steinem, however, the issue of women's rights was now all too real. Reading all she could about women's history and women's lives, she began to realize just how oppressed women were. "I began to learn from other women, to figure out the politics of my own life, and to experiment with telling the truth in public. That was the beginning," she remembered.

An 1869 cartoon (top) ridicules the efforts of American women seeking the right to vote. In 1912, women take to the streets of New York (bottom), still demanding the vote. American women did not achieve suffrage until 1920.

The First Wave of Feminism

The feminist movement that began in the late 1960s has been called the "second wave" of feminism. The first wave took place in the nineteenth century, when suffragists demanded equal rights for women. The most notable leaders included Elizabeth Cady Stanton (1818–1893), Susan B. Anthony (1820–1906), and Lucretia Mott (1793–1880). In July 1848, they held the first Women's Rights Convention in Seneca Falls, New York. In addition to women's rights, they worked to abolish slavery and secure voting rights for African Americans. This first wave of feminists achieved one of their major goals in 1920 with the passage of the Nineteenth Amendment to the U.S. Constitution, which gave women the right to vote.

Steinem was certainly not the only woman who had awakened to feminism at that time. Increasingly, young women who had not been moved by the more conservative, traditional approach of NOW were coming together in small groups to discuss their lives. They practiced **consciousness raising**, talking together about their day-to-day experiences, which raised their political and social awareness and created connections among them. Like people in the civil rights and student antiwar movements—in which many of these women had been active—they held sit-ins and protests. They proclaimed, "the personal is political" and "sisterhood is powerful." In other words, even everyday concerns—such as who did the housework and who cared for the children—were significant issues to be addressed, and if women joined together, they could bring about change.

GOING ON THE ROAD FOR FEMINISM

While Steinem became more involved with feminism, she continued to write for New York magazine. In the summer of 1969, she attended a weekend meeting of Democratic politicians and realized that the men did not consider women or their problems to be important. (Many men did not consider feminism to be significant at the time, but as the movement grew, some would feel threatened by the changes feminism promised to bring.) Writing in New York, Steinem stated: "I realize that, unless women organize, support each other, and force change, nothing basic is going to happen. Not even with the best of men." It was time to begin meeting with other women on a large scale.

Steinem had recently written a column about Dorothy Pitman Hughes, a young African-American woman who ran a New York child care center. When

Steinem was invited to give a speech about the women's movement at New York University, she asked Hughes to join her. Steinem had a great fear of speaking to large groups in public, and she felt having a partner would make speaking easier. Soon after, she was asked to speak on college campuses around the country, and again she wanted Hughes with her. It was important to Steinem that her speaking partner be African American. Many women felt feminism was chiefly a movement of educated, middle-class, white women. Steinem wanted to appeal to all women: young and old, rich and poor, heterosexual and gay, and of all races and ethnic groups.

Throughout the early 1970s, Steinem traveled a great deal to lecture about the women's movement. Her speaking companion was usually an African-American woman—first Hughes, and then attorney and activist Florynce Kennedy as well as writer and organizer Margaret Sloan. Although Steinem and her partners sometimes met with hostility, they continued to speak, anxious to reach women who had not yet been affected by feminism. They talked about issues such as abortion, child care, equal pay for women performing the same work as men, and the Equal Rights Amendment being considered by the U.S. Congress.

Steinem confers with an African American colleague during the 1972 Democratic presidential convention. She wanted feminism to appeal to women of all races and economic classes.

The Equal Rights Amendment

The Equal Rights Amendment was a proposed amendment to the U.S. Constitution that stated: "Equality of rights under the law shall not be denied or abridged by the United States or by any state on account of sex." The ERA was introduced in Congress a number of times and finally passed in March 1972, after which it went to the states for approval. When it failed to receive approval from the necessary number of states, a huge rally was held in Washington, D.C., in July 1978 to ask Congress for an extension of the deadline. The deadline was extended, but the ERA failed on June 30, 1982, still three states short of approval. An organized effort to defeat the ERA had been mounted by conservative groups who felt that the amendment—and feminism in general—threatened women's traditional roles as wives and mothers and the family as the basic unit of society.

More important than the lectures themselves were the discussions that followed, when women spoke about their own lives. During these give-and-take sessions, women of different backgrounds discovered they shared many of the same experiences. They also realized they were strong and capable and deserved the rights they had demanded. Steinem reflected years later, "I was seeing women flower and change in a miraculous way that continues on a far larger scale now, but was then a surprise every day, from the first sanity-saving 'I am not alone' to the talent-freeing discovery 'I am unique.' . . .

Steinem (top, far left) holds hands with other supporters of the ERA during a 1978 march in Washington, D.C., urging Congress to extend the deadline for ratification. The ERA had some staunch opponents, including Phyllis Schlafly (bottom, right), leader of the group STOP ERA.

At a 1970 press conference, Steinem speaks with feminist author Kate Millett. The media portrayed Steinem as a symbol for the women's movement, making her a well-known figure.

The most important thing we did was to make a space for women to come together . . . and hear experiences confirmed by each other's lives."

A GREATER PUBLIC ROLE

As the women's movement continued to grow, Steinem's role grew with it. On August 26, 1970, demonstrations were held nationwide in a Women's Strike for Equality, organized by Betty Friedan on the fiftieth anniversary of women's suffrage. Friedan led some fifty thousand people in a march up New York City's Fifth Avenue. At a rally before the march, Steinem stated the march's goals—better child care, fairness in jobs and education, and reproductive rights. She was at the head of the march and introduced the speakers featured at a rally that ended the day's events.

In July 1971, Steinem joined other feminist leaders—including Friedan and two U.S. congresswomen

from New York, Bella Abzug and Shirley Chisholm—in founding the National Women's Political Caucus. The group included women from both major political parties. Its goals were to help elect women to political offices and get women more involved at all levels of public life.

Feminists were making progress, but they knew they had a difficult road ahead. They were challenging some of American society's basic ideas about the roles of men and women. Feminists were often criticized for being too aggressive, and they were portrayed as crazy "women's libbers" ("lib" being short for liberation) and "bra burners" (to protest what they considered male-dominated notions of how women should dress, some feminists burned their bras). If many men opposed feminism, so did many women. They wanted to keep their roles as housewives and mothers, and they feared equality would lead to women being drafted by the military and losing financial support from their husbands.

At this time, the media began portraying Steinem as a symbol for the women's movement, as well as one of its leaders. This media attention was partly due to her appearance. With her short skirts, streaked hair, and stylish aviator glasses, Steinem was an attractive woman. She didn't look like the **stereotype** of a feminist—drab, strict, and serious—and she didn't act like one, either. Many people believed feminists hated men. But Steinem liked men, and men—including those in the media—liked her. In August 1971, Newsweek put her on its cover for a story entitled "The New Woman."

Steinem's fame bothered many feminists, who noted that she seemed to be getting all the credit while others who had long been active in the movement received none. Some feminists didn't think the movement needed a leader at all. Steinem soon proved, however, just how important she could be to the cause of feminism.

Steinem meeting with members of the *Ms.* staff

SPEARHEADING THE MOVEMENT

In the discussions that followed Steinem's lectures, women always asked many practical questions, such as how to find a good child care center, receive counseling after a rape, or reenter the work force after years of staying at home. In early 1971, Steinem and attorney Brenda Feigen Fasteau began a research and referral organization called the Women's Action Alliance to provide information on these questions and others. The alliance also planned to help fund local action projects, such as training programs for jobs normally closed to women and drives to adopt textbooks that were not **sexist** in public schools.

Such an organization, however, could provide information only on a limited scale. Many women were still not connected to the movement, so Steinem invited a number of writers and activists to her apartment to explore new ways to reach more women. They concluded that women needed a national feminist publication that was run by women. The idea for Ms. magazine was born.

Patricia Carbine (left), the publisher of *Ms.*, and Steinem pose in front of an enlarged cover of the magazine's fifth-anniversary issue in 1977.

THE BIRTH OF MS.

The Ms. project came together quickly, since many women wanted to be involved with the new magazine. Patricia Carbine, the editor of

McCall's and the highest ranking woman in magazine publishing, agreed to leave her job and join Ms. A major problem—finding enough money to begin publication—was solved by Steinem's old friend Clay Felker, the editor of New York magazine. He suggested that Ms. begin as a special insert in the year-end issue of New York in December 1971. Then, in exchange for a share of the profits, New York would help fund the 128-page preview issue of Ms. that would appear on its own in January 1972.

The preview issue of Ms. had a cover that featured a painting of a blue-skinned, eight-armed woman. She had tears running down her face, and each of her hands held the objects that defined a housewife's life: telephone, mirror, steering wheel, iron, clock, feather duster, frying pan, and typewriter. Women were clearly struck by the cover—as well as by the magazine's contents. Three hundred thousand copies of the preview issue had been printed. They were supposed to be on sale for two months, but they sold out in eight days.

FULFILLING A NEED

Ms. obviously filled a real need. Many women did not want another magazine full of recipes, fashion, and beauty columns. In Ms., they were pleased to discover a forum for feminist ideas and trends, with interviews, history, fiction, and poetry, as well as down-to-earth articles. They also appreciated the lack of sexist advertisements that degraded women. (The magazine's refusal to accept such ads, however, meant that it was always short of money, even though it had many subscribers.) Ms. could be controversial. The preview issue, for example, included a two-page declaration, "We have had abortions," at a time when abortion was still illegal in the

The Preview Issue of *Ms.*

The preview issue of *Ms.* contained a range of articles, including an emotional piece by Steinem called "Sisterhood." The articles gave a clear indication of what kind of topics the magazine intended to explore:

"Down with Sexist Upbringing"

"Why Women Fear Success"

"The Housewife's Moment of Truth"

"How to Write Your Own Marriage Contract"

"The Black Family and Feminism"

"Welfare Is a Women's Issue"

"Can Women Love Women?"

United States. It was signed by Steinem and fifty-two other prominent women, including tennis star Billie Jean King, singer Judy Collins, and writer Lillian Hellman.

Many doubted the magazine would survive. After the appearance of the first regular issue—dated July 1972, with the comic book hero Wonder Woman on the cover—television journalist Harry Reasoner declared, "I give it six months before they run out of things to say." Yet they never did. For the next fifteen years, under Steinem's leadership, Ms. continued to publish thought-provoking

The cover of the preview issue of *Ms.* magazine

articles on a range of controversial topics—domestic violence, sexual harassment, equal pay for comparable work, alternatives to **mastectomy** in cases of breast cancer, pornography, date rape, incest—as well as useful stories on how to conduct a consciousness-raising group, fix a car, and examine one's own body.

The Mood at *Ms.*

The *Ms.* office could seem chaotic and disorganized. There was little hierarchy. Every woman was called an editor, no matter what she did, and instead of having separate offices, almost every employee had a desk (painted the color of her choice) in a large, open space. Anyone could attend editorial meetings and offer ideas, and articles were edited by groups of five or six. Mary Thom, who worked at *Ms.* for many years, described the magazine's early days:

To some degree, everyone there was acquiring, or sharpening, a feminist consciousness in daily . . . on-the-job training. . . . Then, as today, feminism was not an ideology set in stone, but rather an adaptable set of attitudes and beliefs. Not only at Ms. *but at school and work, within homes and neighborhoods, women were making it up as they went along.*

POLITICS—NOT AS USUAL

As Ms. became the voice of feminism, Steinem continued to be seen by many as the movement's leader. In 1972, she was busier than ever. She edited Ms., traveled and lectured, and in July acted as a spokesperson for the National Women's Political Caucus at the Democratic presidential convention in Miami, Florida. Women made up an unprecedented 40 percent of the delegates and

Wherever Steinem traveled, she met women who shared experiences and forged important bonds, supporting each other as they worked for social change.

played many key roles at the convention. Although the women's proposal on abortion rights was defeated, the issue was debated for the first time at a national political convention, and the platform of the Democratic Party included many issues critical to women.

The following years were filled with political activity. Steinem worked for the passage of the ERA and helped plan the women's agenda for the 1976 Democratic convention. In November 1977, she played an active role in the National Women's Conference in Houston, Texas, attended by some twenty thousand women of all races and social and economic groups. The conference—the first of its kind—produced a National Plan of Action that covered a broad range of women's issues. Steinem later called her main job at the conference—helping to write the minority women's plank—the "emotional highlight" of her twenty years as a writer.

The publicity Steinem was receiving continued to create resentment among many feminists, and it eventually led to some negative media attention. Betty Friedan had been upset in 1972 when the National Women's Political Caucus chose Steinem over her as its spokesperson, and Friedan had criticized Steinem. She told one college audience, "The media tries to make her a celebrity, but no one should mistake her for a leader." Friedan's comments were a prime example of what came to be known in the feminist movement as "trashing"—the sad tendency for women to undermine other women by verbally attacking them. The media played up the apparent feud between these two leading feminists, but Steinem took no part in it.

At the 1972 Democratic presidential convention, Steinem nominated Texas legislator Frances "Sissy" Farenthold for vice president, making Farenthold the first woman to be nominated for that position.

In 1975, Friedan joined other feminists in criticizing Steinem after the Redstockings, the radical feminist group, claimed Steinem had ties to the Central Intelligence Agency. The Redstockings announced that the Independent Research Service—the group Steinem had worked for in the late 1950s—was funded by the CIA, and that moreover, Steinem was still working for the agency. Steinem admitted that the CIA had connections to the Independent Research Service, but she said she did not know about the connections when she worked for the group. She denied that she still worked for the CIA, but the accusation hurt her deeply.

THE LONGEST OF ALL REVOLUTIONS

The late 1970s and 1980s were a difficult period for Steinem. Her mother, Ruth, died in 1981. Ruth had done fairly well after being hospitalized in the late 1950s for treatment of her mental illness, at times living independently and other times living with Steinem's sister, Susanne, and Susanne's family. Steinem wrote her emotional essay "Ruth's Song" after Ruth's death to come to grips with her loss and to understand better the difficulties of Ruth's life. The essay was included in Steinem's first book, a collection of essays entitled Outrageous Acts and Everyday Rebellions. It was published in 1983 and became a best-seller.

Outrageous Acts

The title of Steinem's book *Outrageous Acts and Everyday Rebellions* came from something she says to her audiences. She urges people to "commit an outrageous act in the cause of simple justice" within twenty-four hours—something as minor as telling someone to "pick it up yourself"—and in so doing, eventually change their lives and the world.

During this period, in what came to be called a "backlash," the feminist movement came under attack from those who believed it was too radical. Ms. also had its troubles, as the magazine struggled to attract advertisers. In the late 1970s, with the magazine deeply in debt, Steinem and Patricia Carbine applied for not-for-profit status from the federal government to help control expenses. Ms. received this status in 1979, but the magazine continued to have financial problems. Beginning in the 1980s, it was sold to a series of different publishers. They limited Steinem's role in the magazine and were not true to the ideals with which she had begun it.

Steinem's fiftieth birthday was celebrated with a dinner and benefit for the Ms. Foundation for Women. Among the celebrities attending were (from left) television personality Phil Donahue and actress Marlo Thomas, shown here with Steinem and her longtime companion Stan Pottinger.

AN UNSUITABLE RELATIONSHIP

Steinem's feminist ideals were seriously called into question when she began a relationship with Mortimer Zuckerman, a millionaire real estate developer, in 1984. For years, Steinem had avoided marriage, although she had enjoyed lengthy relationships with various men. One was Franklin Thomas, an African-American attorney who became head of the Ford Foundation. Another was Stan Pottinger, a liberal Justice Department lawyer younger than she was who was divorced and had two

Mortimer Zuckerman. Steinem had a four-year relationship with Zuckerman, a wealthy real estate developer who did not share her political beliefs and social values.

Avoiding Marriage

Steinem long thought that she would eventually marry and have children, yet she kept avoiding marriage. In her book *Revolution from Within: A Book of Self-Esteem* (1992), she wrote about her realization that it was all right to remain unmarried and that she could be happy as she was:

Fortunately, feminism came along to help me and millions of others try to become ourselves, with or without marriage; to understand, in the brilliant phrase of some anonymous feminist, that we could "become the men we wanted to marry." I realized that everyone didn't have to live the same way, and this led to a more personal discovery: I was happy.

young children. Before Zuckerman, all of Steinem's companions shared her political beliefs. But Zuckerman represented a change. Steinem described him as "a man different from others I had known."

Zuckerman was not concerned with Steinem's activities, interests, or friends, and he did not support her causes. At this point in her life, however, Steinem was feeling particularly tired and stressed. Zuckerman provided a comfortable, even luxurious, lifestyle, caring for Steinem physically—if not emotionally—when she needed it. The relationship, which ended in 1988, caused Steinem to question why she had been "so attracted to someone so obviously wrong for me."

TURNING INWARD

In 1986, Steinem was diagnosed with breast cancer, which was treated with a **lumpectomy** and radiation treatment. She beat the cancer, but her illness forced her to recognize how unhealthy her lifestyle had been, with its frequent stress, constant travel, sleeplessness, lack of exercise, and poor eating habits. Changing how she lived, she began taking better care of herself and devoted more time to her writing. She also realized that she had virtually no savings, no health insurance, and not even a comfortable place to live. Steinem unpacked the cartons she had lived with for years. After buying the apartment below the one she already owned, she turned both into one large living space. She even bought a cat.

She also began seeing a therapist in an effort to deal with her past. Therapy helped her understand that she had never been allowed to be a child because she had been forced into a care-giving role for her mother, and that she kept repeating patterns from her past, such as tolerating instability in her life and not caring for herself. She also realized that her writing had become "calm, intellectualized, impersonal." Steinem's experiences with therapy led her to write Revolution from Within: A Book of Self-Esteem (1992). A best-seller, the book focused on becoming aware of one's inner life and using knowledge of one's past to help shape one's future.

Steinem returned to Ms. as a consulting editor in 1990, when it began appearing as a bimonthly, ad-free publication fully supported by its readers. After the magazine was sold again in 1998, its new owners suspended publication. Then, Liberty Media for Women—a group of feminists that included Steinem—bought Ms. and began publishing it again. The group was itself bought by the Feminist Majority Foundation, a feminist research and action organization, in 2001. The magazine celebrated its thirtieth anniversary in the spring of 2002, and featured Steinem on the cover.

In September 2000, Steinem surprised everyone by getting married, at the age

Steinem marches in a 1996 parade sponsored by NOW.

The thirtieth-anniversary issue of *Ms.*, with Steinem on the cover

SPECIAL! COLLECTORS ISSUE   AFGHAN WOMEN • A FEMINIST FAMILY

Ms.

VOLUME XII NUMBER 2 • SPRING 2002 • U.S. $5.95 CANADA $6.95

the best of

30 years

Reporting Rebelling & Truth-telling

of sixty-six. The groom was David Bale, a South African-born businessman. She commented after the wedding, "Though I've worked many years to make marriage more equal, I never expected to take advantage of it myself. I'm happy, surprised and one day will write about it, but for now, I hope this proves what feminists have always said—that feminism is about the ability to choose what's right at each time in our lives."

Steinem and her husband, David Bale, in 2001

"IN IT FOR LIFE"

Steinem is now at an age when most people think about retirement or have already retired. Yet she is still going strong and notes that she has become even more radical. Despite the advances women have made in the last thirty years, the feminist movement—which Steinem has called "this longest of all revolutions"—is not over yet.

The U.S. workforce now includes more than 65 million women, but on average they still earn far less than men performing comparable work. Even successful women executives often face the "glass ceiling"—an invisible barrier that prevents women and minorities from rising to the highest positions in the business world. Women make up a

higher proportion of people living in poverty, face problems such as sexual harassment, and continue to fight for their reproductive rights. Since women still do most of the work at home, many are under considerable pressure to balance demanding jobs with the responsibilities of home and family. "In my first days of activism," Steinem once wrote, "I thought I would do this ('this' being feminism) for a few years and then return to my real life. . . . I've learned that this is not just something we care about for a year or two or three. We are in it for life—and for our lives."

Steinem has never stopped speaking on women's issues. She also campaigns for candidates she believes in and continues to be active in various organizations

The first regular issue of *Ms.* featured Wonder Woman on the cover. Steinem read Wonder Woman comics as a child, and she was influenced by the strong female character.

Women in the United States have made many advances in the past thirty years. In 1983, physicist Sally Ride (below, left) became the first American woman to travel in space. The Women's National Basketball Association (WNBA) has been drawing fans since play began in 1997. Below, right, players clash during the 2002 WNBA finals.

Take Our Daughters to Work Day

In 1993—concerned with evidence that girls' self-esteem dropped as they became older—the Ms. Foundation for Women began Take Our Daughters to Work Day. For one day each April, parents were urged to bring their daughters into the workplace, so girls could see that they could become judges, NASA engineers, construction workers, or whatever else they wanted. In 2002, the Ms. Foundation announced that, beginning in 2003, the program would be called Take Our Daughters & Sons to Work Day. "We are making this change because revolution demands evolution," the president of the foundation explained, going on to say that the new program would help "girls and boys . . . learn to work together to bring about a more equitable world—at home, at school and in the workplace."

In 1981, Sandra Day O'Connor was sworn in as a U.S. Supreme Court justice, becoming the first woman in U.S. history to serve on the Court. A second woman, Ruth Bader Ginsburg, joined the Court in 1993.

she helped found, such as the Coalition of Labor Union Women and Voters for Choice (a group that supports pro-choice political candidates).

Her personal revolution still continues as well. When she approached her sixtieth birthday, Steinem wrote an essay entitled "Doing Sixty." In it, she states: "Age is supposed to create more serenity, calm, and detachment from the world, right? Well, I'm feeling just the reverse. The older I get, the more intensely I feel about the world around me. . . . Some of this journey's content is uniquely mine, and I find excitement in its solitary, edge-of-the-world sensation of entering new territory with the wind whistling past my ears." Gloria Steinem is still entering new territory every day.

Steinem, shown with former U.S. vice president and presidential candidate Al Gore, continues to campaign for politicians she believes in, and she is active in a number of political organizations she helped found.

TIMELINE

1934	Gloria Marie Steinem is born on March 25 in Toledo, Ohio
1944	Begins living with her emotionally disturbed mother after her parents separate
1951	Moves to Washington, D.C., where she finishes high high school
1956	Graduates Smith College; has abortion in England
1957	Studies, travels, and writes in India on a fellowship
1958	Works for Independent Research Service
1960	Moves to New York City to become a writer
1963	Publishes two-part series of articles about going undercover as a Playboy Bunny; publishes *The Beach Book*; participates in civil rights March on Washington
1968	Becomes a contributing editor and political columnist for *New York* magazine
1969	Attends speakout on abortion; becomes involved with feminism
1970	Begins speaking on feminism around the country; participates in Women's Strike for Equality on August 26
1971	Steinem helps found the National Women's Political Caucus and the Women's Action Alliance; *Ms.* appears as a special insert in *New York* magazine in December
1972	Preview issue of *Ms.* is published in January and first regular issue in July; Steinem acts as spokesperson for the National Women's Political Caucus at the Democratic presidential convention in Miami, Florida
1975	Criticized by Redstockings for alleged involvement with CIA
1977	Participates in the National Women's Conference in Houston, Texas
1983	*Outrageous Acts and Everyday Rebellions* is published
1986	Receives treatment for breast cancer
1992	*Revolution from Within: A Book of Self-Esteem* is published
1994	*Moving Beyond Words* is published
2000	Marries David Bale

GLOSSARY

abortion: a procedure that ends a pregnancy by removing the embryo or fetus from the womb.

castes: in India, social classes that people are born into and remain within for their entire lives, and which are defined by degrees of wealth and status.

civil rights: the basic rights belonging to every citizen in a country.

communists: people who believe a government should own all or most property and should control the economy.

consciousness raising: the act of increasing one's awareness of an issue through discussion and debate.

feminism: a movement that seeks rights and opportunities for women equal to those of men.

forum: a publication or place where ideas can be exchanged.

incest: sexual activity between close relatives; it is prohibited in most cultures and is a crime in the United States.

lumpectomy: a treatment for breast cancer that involves removing just the tumor and sometimes adjacent tissue.

mastectomy: a treatment for breast cancer that involves removing the breast.

migrant: a person, such as a farm worker, who moves from place to place.

Nazis: members of a political party in Germany that was led by Adolf Hitler from 1921 to 1945.

pornography: material, such as films and magazines, that has the sole purpose of causing sexual excitement.

rape: the crime of having sex with a person against the person's will.

sexist: believing in stereotypes based on gender, or displaying attitudes or behaviors that foster those stereotypes.

sexual harassment: unwanted sexual advances toward a person, especially by someone who has authority over that person.

stereotype: a simplistic view of a particular group of people, often based on gender, race, ethnicity, or religion.

sterilization: a medical procedure that makes a person unable to have children.

suffrage: the right to vote.

TO FIND OUT MORE

BOOKS

Bjornlund, Lydia D. *Women of the Suffrage Movement (Women in History)*. San Diego: Lucent Books, 2003.

Heinemann, Sue. *The New York Public Library Amazing Women in American History: A Book of Answers for Kids.* New York: Wiley, 1998.

Keenan, Sheila. *Scholastic Encyclopedia of Women in the United States.* New York: Scholastic, 2002.

Lazo, Caroline Evenson. *Gloria Steinem: Feminist Extraordinaire (Newsmakers Biographies).* Minneapolis: Lerner Publications, 1998.

Ross, Mandy. *The Changing Role of Women (20th Century Perspectives).* Crystal Lake, IL.: Heinemann Library, 2002.

Steinem, Gloria. *Outrageous Acts and Everyday Rebellions.* New York: Holt, 1995.

Wheaton, Elizabeth. *Ms.: The Story of Gloria Steinem (Feminist Voices).* Greensboro, N.C.: Morgan Reynolds, 2002.

INTERNET SITES

Glass Ceiling Biographies
www.theglassceiling.com/biographies/bio32.htm
A biography of Gloria Steinem, plus links to the stories of other famous women.

Ms. Magazine Online
www.msmagazine.com
Current and past issues of *Ms.*, as well as information on topics of interest to women and the history of the magazine.

National Women's Hall of Fame
www.greatwomen.org
Official site of the National Women's Hall of Fame in Seneca Falls, New York, with biographies of all the women inducted into the Hall, including Gloria Steinem.

Women's History Month
www.galegroup.com/free_resources/whm
Includes biographies of Gloria Steinem and other notable women, a timeline of important events, and other materials.

INDEX

About the Author

Jacqueline Laks Gorman has been an editor and writer for more than twenty years. A native of Brooklyn, New York, she attended Barnard College (an all-women's school) and received a master's degree in American history from Columbia University. She worked in the publishing industry on a broad range of nonfiction and reference books before becoming a freelance editor and writer in 1991. She currently lives in DeKalb, Illinois, with her husband, David, and children, Colin and Caitlin. She still owns her copy of the preview issue of Ms. that she bought in 1972.